FIFTY

50 years 50 species

**Berkshire
Buckinghamshire
Oxfordshire**

Champions for wildlife – Berks, Bucks and Oxon Wildlife Trust

Berks, Bucks & Oxon Wildlife Trust,
The Lodge, 1 Armstrong Road, Littlemore, Oxford OX4 4XT
Tel: 01865 775476
Email: info@bbowt.org.uk
www.bbowt.org.uk

Berkshire
Buckinghamshire
Oxfordshire

First published 2010

British-Library-in-Publication Data
A catalogue record for this book is available from the British Library

ISBN 978-1-874357-43-8

Edited by Helen Walsh

Designed and published for BBOWT by Pisces Publications

Pisces Publications is the imprint of NatureBureau, 36 Kingfisher Court,
Hambridge Road, Newbury, Berkshire RG14 5SJ
www.naturebureau.co.uk

Printed and bound in China by 1010 Printing International Ltd

Front cover: Badger (Andy Rouse/nhpa)
Back cover: View from Bowdown Woods Nature Reserve (Rob Appleby)
Legacy page: Barn owl (John Waters/naturepl.com)

Treasuring wildlife

Sleepy hamlets amongst gently rolling hills may not seem to be the place for intrigue and phantasmagoric spectacle, but here in the Chilterns, Thames Valley and surrounding heaths, marshes and meadows, a magical, natural wonderland bustles and thrums its way through the year. For me, the seasons are embodied in an image from my treasured home counties; a bluebell wood with floating brimstone butterflies in spring, the sounds of sunrise over wildflower meadows in summer, the damp smell of a mossy woodland after rain in autumn and the whistling soaring of red kites over a mist-laced river in winter.

The natural world is infinite in its complexity and changing character, and the return of the familiar brings me as much joy as the discovery of the new or unexpected. We are so lucky to be living in this sleepy corner of the country, where a Sunday afternoon trundle can put you into a sublime English country idyll straight out of the pages of Hardy or Wordsworth. As a child I hankered after the exotic, to chase snakes through the Amazon and dive with sea monsters, but the more I lived out my dreams, the more I came to truly appreciate what had been staring me in the face for all those years. The shy sprouting of a tiny orchid on the edge of a woodland, the unexpected grandeur of one of our multitude of sphinx moths, a barn owl flashing through the headlights at dusk like a phantom… I could go on and on and on.

"As a child I hankered after the exotic, but the more I lived out my dreams, the more I came to truly appreciate what had been staring me in the face: the shy sprouting of a tiny orchid, the unexpected grandeur of a sphinx moth, a barn owl flashing through the headlights … I could go on and on and on."

Of course, though I might tell a thousand tales of bliss, the wildlife in our patch is under threat from all sides, and it's our job as enthusiasts of the natural world to do our bit to protect it. Without the work of the Berks, Bucks & Oxon Wildlife Trust (BBOWT), wildlife in our three counties would be so much poorer. This is testament to the hard work of volunteers and staff over the last 50 years, and the generous support of our members and the public from young to old. The wild world has a unique power to heal, to enthuse, to fill to bursting with joy: a fact I fondly hope the next generation will discover as we have. Of course the only way they can do that is if we make sure our wild places and wildlife are looked after for years to come…

Here's to the next 50 years!

Steve Backshall, BBOWT Vice President and BBC presenter

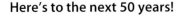

College Lake Nature Reserve

Champions for local wildlife

Just over 50 years ago, a small group of people met one November evening in a school hall in the middle of Oxford. The actions they agreed to take that evening mean that today, in our three counties, we can still enjoy a whole host of delightful, often spectacular and certainly well-loved native wild plants and animals in their natural habitats.

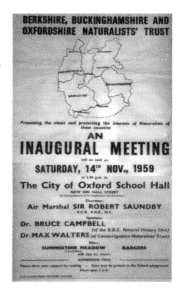

If that small band of naturalists had not had a deep knowledge of the natural world, they would not have understood how badly things were going wrong with the management of our countryside at the time. But they had been watching the massive intensification of farming and the indiscriminate development of the countryside, and in doing so witnessed the devastating consequences for wildlife. They knew something needed to be done urgently, before many species disappeared altogether, and they were prepared to commit themselves to work towards halting such needless destruction of our wild places and wildlife. And so the local Wildlife Trust was born.

The newly created BBONT (we were then a Naturalists' Trust) soon realised that wildlife needed a strong champion to help affect long-overdue change in order to save it. This change included: bringing some of the most fragile and precious habitats under their ownership and turning them into nature reserves; influencing policy makers locally and nationally to provide protection for the most threatened species and habitats, and making sure that the next generation understood the value of the natural world and was prepared to form the next wave of wildlife guardians.

The next generation

Fifty years on from those pioneering days, we are that next generation and we have a huge amount to thank those founder members for; this book is a tribute to them. Sadly, most are no longer with us, but their legacy lives on as BBOWT now protects 80 nature reserves and cares for wildlife across the wider countryside, supported by over 50,000 members and hundreds of volunteers.

As you turn the pages of this beautiful book – a celebration of our 50th anniversary – we hope you will not only be awed by the sheer beauty of the animals and plants that live in our region, but that you'll be surprised and pleased by the ways in which BBOWT has been instrumental in helping to protect this natural beauty. We have chosen just 50 species to showcase here, but it could so easily have been 500, if only we had the space within these pages… There are just so many fabulous stories to tell!

"A small band of naturalists committed themselves to work towards halting the needless destruction of our wild places and wildlife. And so the local Wildlife Trust was born."

"There are so many people we'd like to thank for our successful 50 years of safeguarding wildlife. This book is an expression of our unending gratitude to all those who have provided so much in terms of effort and financial support over the years."

It would have been a very different story had BBOWT never existed. No doubt certain sites and species would still have had their champions. But over 50 years, BBOWT has been able to harness so much local knowledge and so many skills, and engage with so many different partners, that we've had a positive impact on the future of local wildlife.

Looking forward

As we look forward to the challenges of the next 50 years, our great hope is that these species not only survive but thrive. With this as our aspiration for the world our children and grandchildren will inherit from us, we certainly have no room for complacency. As biodiversity continues to decline both locally, nationally and indeed internationally, the Wildlife Trusts across the UK have a new rallying cry. We know we cannot just keep on doing more of the same and watch our precious nature reserves become more and more isolated – little oases for wildlife surrounded by hostile and barren wildlife 'deserts'. And we know that safeguarding biodiversity is not just about saving a collection of species either; a healthy ecosystem provides us with the essentials for life – clean water, rich and fertile soils for food production, reduced carbon emissions and a healthy environment in which we can recharge our batteries.

So, once again, we are calling for change. This time to recognise and protect much larger areas, where pockets of habitat can be linked together to form a giant patchwork of natural spaces, allowing wildlife to move about freely. Working on this landscape scale means creating 'living landscapes' – places where wildlife can thrive and people can enjoy the benefits of a healthy ecosystem.

We can only achieve this vision in partnership with many other organisations. But even more importantly, with the support of local people who understand that a future rich in wildlife is also the best possible way of securing our own future wellbeing on this little green planet.

A thank you

There are so many people we'd like to thank for our successful 50 years of safeguarding the wildlife portrayed within this book – too many to mention individually. To name one or two would be to miss out hundreds of others. This book is an expression of our unending gratitude to all those who have provided so much in terms of effort and financial support over many years. We look forward to it continuing long into the future as we champion wildlife for the next 50 years.

Philippa Lyons, Chief Executive

West Berkshire Living Landscape

Acknowledgements

Special thanks go to Peter Creed who was inspired to create this beautiful book and who has donated many hours of his time and expertise to bring together such an exquisite collection of images in a stunning format.

Thanks also go to the photographers who donated their wildlife images as part of this special project; David Kjaer, in particular, has been gracious in giving us access to his amazing collection of photos. Other contributors to thank include Rob Appleby, Jim Asher, Peter Creed, Kate Dent, Andy Fairbairn, David Green, Gavin Hageman, Kerry Lock, Terry Longley, James Osmond and Helen Walsh.

We'd also like to thank Mandy Brilliant for her commitment to detail when proofreading this book.

Bowdown Woods Nature Reserve

Special places for wildlife – BBOWT's best nature reserves

Key

● **Hartslock**
BBOWT nature reserves
mentioned in this book

● Other BBOWT
nature reserves

Little Linford Wood

Banbury

Milton Keynes

Hook Norton Cutting

Chipping Norton

Buckingham

Pilch Field

BUCKS

Bicester

Finemere Wood

Woodsides Meadow

Upper Ray Meadows

Whitecross Green Wood

Rushbeds Wood

College Lake

Asham Meads

Aston Clinton Ragpits

Aylesbury

Burford

Oxey Mead

Sydlings Copse

Bernwood Meadows

Weston Turville Reservoir

Dancersend

Foxholes

Witney

OXON

Oxford

Thame

Lashford Lane Fen

Chimney Meadows

Iffley Meadows

Chinnor Hill

Amersham

Parsonage Moor

Wells Farm

Hitchcopse Pit

Dry Sandford Pit

Abingdon

High Wycombe

Wantage

Wallingford

Warburg

Marlow

Beaconsfield

Didcot

Homefield Wood

Haymill Valley

Warren Bank

Maidenhead

Slough

Hartslock

Henley-on-Thames

Moor Copse

Loddon

Windsor

Reading

BERKS

Hungerford

Bracknell

Kintbury Newt Ponds

Thatcham

Hungerford Marsh

Newbury

Bowdown Woods

Wokingham

Wildmoor Heath

Inkpen Common

Decoy Heath

1
∾ ADDER ∾

To see a tightly coiled adder basking in the spring sunshine, fresh and bright after shedding its skin, is a rare treat for the nature-lover these days. Adders were once quite common across heaths, grasslands and woods, but have suffered serious declines mainly due to the loss and fragmentation of their habitat. They were also routinely persecuted in years gone by, but thankfully, are now legally protected.

In our region, Berkshire is the stronghold for this enigmatic creature, with populations at Bowdown Woods, Decoy Heath and Wildmoor Heath nature reserves. But it is Warburg Nature Reserve which could be the last remaining refuge for adders in Oxfordshire. Here, careful habitat management during the winter ensures that basking sites remain open to the sun, but still provide some shelter from predators; while new, warm basking spots have been constructed from logs and branches – perfect for a spot of sun-bathing!

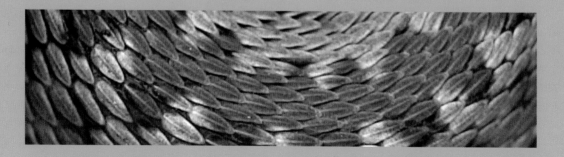

2
◦ BADGER ◦

The badger, a distinctive mammal with a famous black and white striped face, has a controversial history. A strong adversary, they were once pitted against fighting dogs for sport. And although the badger now has legal protection, this practice still continues.

Recently, the badger has been framed as the main culprit for the spread of bovine tuberculosis in cattle. There have been widespread calls for badger culls by worried farmers, but independent evidence has demonstrated that culling can actually help to spread the disease. The Wildlife Trusts are lobbying hard to save the badger from persecution.

Badgers are actually shy, nocturnal creatures which would prefer to keep away from people. Development pressures make that impossible; sadly, as many as 50,000 badgers are killed on roads every year. So BBOWT works to ensure that the welfare of badgers is considered in the planning process. Many of our woodland reserves provide sanctuaries where badgers can live undisturbed – Moor Copse, Finemere Wood and Sydlings Copse, to name but a few.

3
∽ BARN OWL ∽

The much-loved barn owl is a stunning bird of prey with golden, buff colours laced with silver-grey tones. A dawn encounter with a 'ghostly' barn owl, gracefully quartering a hay meadow for its next meal, is an image which lasts long in the memory. Barn owls are perfectly adapted to hunt in darkness with deadly precision. The almost silent flight and the characteristic heart-shaped face, which directs high-frequency sounds, enable them to find mice, voles and shrews hidden in deep vegetation.

Throughout history, barn owls have been known by many different names; 'demon owl' in particular illustrating how they were once considered by many rural populations. But this is not so difficult to appreciate if you have ever heard its blood-curdling, screeching call!

BBOWT is helping to reverse the dramatic national decline of this species. At Chimney Meadows, the provision of strategically placed nest boxes and the creation of rough grassland feeding habitat has allowed barn owls to thrive.

4

∽ BLACK HAIRSTREAK ∾

Despite their name, black hairstreaks are actually a soft brown colour that develops a golden sheen in the sunshine. The 'black' part of their name comes from a row of black dots running along the edge of the wing.

These small butterflies fly during midsummer when many other butterfly species are taking a break, but are still often missed by nature-spotters. The black hairstreak is particularly elusive because it spends much of its life perched on the tops of trees and is seldom stirred to take to the wing. Binoculars prove essential to those who wish to see this treetop treasure.

Buckinghamshire and Oxfordshire are especially important for this species as, across Britain, it is only present on the clay belt between Oxford and Peterborough. Black hairstreak caterpillars are almost entirely dependent on blackthorn, so careful management of this scrubby plant in BBOWT's woodlands and hedgerows has ensured that this rare butterfly flourishes on many of our reserves.

5
◦ BLACKENING WAXCAP ◦

Waxcaps, brightly coloured and becoming increasingly uncommon, are found in unimproved grassland and downland. They come in many colours – bright yellow, white, green, orange and vibrant reds. Many are tiny, measuring only one or two centimetres across; others are larger and more impressive, like the blackening waxcap.

Sharply conical, blackening waxcaps push their way through the often hard turf in the late autumn. The colourful, waxy caps vary from yellow-orange to bright red, eventually splitting and turning up at the edge. As they age, the brightly coloured caps start to blacken and eventually become entirely black, hence the name.

Waxcap grasslands are not a familiar sight nowadays as many have been lost or 'improved' by fertilisers. Luckily, BBOWT protects several areas on its nature reserves where these delightful little fungi thrive. Chinnor Hill in Oxfordshire is one such place, as is the small meadow within Bowdown Woods in Berkshire, where several waxcap species grow.

6

⟿ BLUEBELL ⟿

What better sight can there be in spring than one of Britain's favourite wildflowers carpeting the woodland floor? Yet, in the not-so-distant past, when forests were seen as forbidding places, it was said that the bluebells would ring out to summon fairies and if you heard these bells, you would die.

There are actually 11 known species of bluebell in the world, but only one is native in Britain, where populations of our bluebell make up 25–50% of the world's total. Our bluebells are under threat, however, from loss of woodlands, hybridisation with the Spanish bluebell (also growing in Britain), collection and illegal sale, and climate change.

Their future is not all doom and gloom though. As well as being afforded legal protection, they are present on many BBOWT nature reserves. At Foxholes, management of the woodland, including scrub-cutting and coppicing, helps to look after the habitat for all kinds of creatures, as well as maintaining the spectacular show of bluebells.

7
∽ BULLFINCH ∾

The bullfinch is one of our most attractive woodland edge birds, but it's had a bad reputation since the 16th century when Henry VIII's condemnation of its 'criminal' attacks on fruit trees led to an Act of Parliament which decreed that one penny would be paid for every bird killed. Bearing rich and colourful plumage, easy to tame and skillful at mimicry, fledglings were also taken for their high value as cage-birds. Luckily, this practice is now outlawed.

Shy and secretive, its peculiar, melancholy call is often the only hint of its presence within the dense, scrubby thicket and untrimmed hedges that it favours. Reserves such as Rushbeds Wood and Whitecross Green Wood are ideal places for bullfinches, which benefit from the sympathetic management of broadleaved and mixed woodland, as well as hedgerow management that encourages dense growth, fruit and seed formation. An orchard creation project at Wells Farm is also providing a haven for these attractive birds.

8

❧ CHALKHILL BLUE ❧

As their name suggests, chalkhill blue butterflies make their home exclusively on chalk downland. Chalk grassland is often referred to as the UK's equivalent of the tropical rainforest, and it is the profusion of wildflowers found growing here which provide an abundant source of food for all kinds of butterflies.

Sadly, the once common sight of clouds of pale blue butterflies zooming from flower to flower on hot summer days is now considered a rare treat. Loss of suitable chalk grassland is a serious problem for these butterflies. And the cold, wet summers we have recently experienced have seriously added to the threats affecting these heat-loving insects.

Many of BBOWT's chalk grassland reserves, such as Hartslock and Aston Clinton Ragpits, remain a haven for chalkhill blues. Careful grazing and scrub control ensures that the perfect conditions are present to support these stunning butterflies.

9

❧ CHILTERN GENTIAN ❧

Our chalk grasslands are truly exquisite in the summer months; all the more so if they have been grazed short by sheep the previous winter. The resulting fine turf shows off the multitude of flowering plants from spring, right through summer, concluding with the proud spikes of the Chiltern gentian. Appearing late in the summer, it provides a welcome splash of royal purple amongst the parched grasses of the chalky soils.

Chiltern gentians are annual or biennial, which means they need to drop their seeds on a suitably bare patch of ground in order to germinate successfully the following year. So, BBOWT uses grazing animals like sheep or cattle to open up the tight grasses and improve their chances of pushing through. Nationally scarce, the Chiltern gentian is a local speciality and there's nowhere better to see the results of the munching endeavours of our roaming livestock than at Chinnor Hill. Here, the Chiltern gentian thrives on the grassland overlooking stunning panoramic views of the Vale of Aylesbury.

10
∽ COMMON FROG ∽

Wet, slimy and fond of lunching on slugs, the common frog may not be the most alluring of creatures, but that hasn't stopped it becoming a firm national favourite and one capable of inspiring generation after generation of new wildlife enthusiasts. Rivalled perhaps only by the transformation of caterpillar to butterfly, the metamorphosis from inky frogspawn dot to wriggling tadpole to amphibious leaping machine has left children in awe of nature for decades. And BBOWT has inspired many generations of nature-lovers with its captivating qualities; pond-dipping a time-tested hit within our educational and outreach work.

As its name suggests, the common frog is widespread in Britain but is also a protected species with a future far from threat-free – a lack of breeding sites is just one hurdle it faces. Thankfully, BBOWT works hard to maintain the habitats so crucial to amphibian survival; at the Upper Ray Meadows alone over 30 new ponds have been created.

11
∾ CORN BUNTING ∾

The corn bunting is a characteristic resident of lowland arable farms and is one of the few British species largely dependent on cropped land. The largest of the buntings, and unassuming in appearance, it is similar to the skylark but with a thicker bill and no crest.

In the summer, corn buntings prefer open farmland where they can often be seen singing; perched prominently on a hedge, post or wire. Their distinctive song sounds like keys jangling in a pocket. In winter, they may be found in stubbles, root crops and weedy fields.

Between 1970 and 2003, corn bunting populations dropped by 89% in the UK. One of the best places to see the corn bunting is Wells Farm where sympathetic management has kept a stable population throughout the national decline. This mixed farm provides corn buntings with seeds from the stubble fields in winter, and plentiful insects and nesting areas in the grassy margins in summer.

12

❧ CORNCOCKLE ❧

Corncockle is one of the more showy members of the specialised group of plants known prosaically as 'arable weeds'. While many of these species were once serious pests of arable crops, a more fitting description would be 'cornfield flowers'.

The corncockle can grow as high as a metre and has large, trumpet-shaped purple flowers. It is so stunning that the old country name for it was 'crown of the fields'. Once common, the seeds made bread bitter or even poisonous if they mixed with wheat. But the increased use of fertilisers and pesticides following the Second World War resulted in the rapid decline of corncockle, which is now extinct in the wild.

At College Lake, things are different. Every summer, a burst of colour can be enjoyed as cornfield flowers thrive on special plots. Arable weed seeds were introduced to the site after being carefully collected by conservationists in the 1980s, and now corncockle is once again the crown of the fields.

13

❧ CURLEW ❧

The evocative sound of the curlew's bubbling display call is unmistakeable, and can be heard on its breeding grounds around the Upper River Ray from mid-February through to early July. In the 1960s, the curlew would have been a common sight flying over the Upper Ray valley. But a 10-year survey conducted during the 1980s revealed a sharp drop in the number of breeding birds – a decline reflected across the country.

In recent years, BBOWT has bought around 130 hectares of land in the Upper Ray area, much of which is suitable habitat for breeding curlew. And in 2009, two pairs nested at Gallows Bridge Farm – a successful start to our management of the site! With the help of neighbouring farmers, agri-environment schemes enabling landowners to afford improvements to their land to benefit wildlife and a firm partnership with the RSPB, curlew numbers now appear to be stable in the area.

14
❧ DARTFORD WARBLER ❧

The diminutive Dartford warbler is almost exclusively found on lowland heathland in the UK, surviving our winters by sheltering amongst the gorse and heather. There are currently around 3,200 pairs, but only 11 pairs survived the especially cold winters of the 1960s. With the unpredictable weather that accompanies climate change, this iconic bird is at risk.

Lowland heathland is an internationally important habitat for the special plants and animals it supports, but it has become fragmented by urban sprawl and agriculture. Linking these pockets of habitat together to form a giant patchwork of natural spaces in which wildlife can move about freely will not only help the Dartford warbler, but many other species too.

BBOWT is leading the way on these landscape-scale projects, one of which encompasses the heathland of Greenham Common – known for its chequered past as an American airbase and the focus for peace demonstrations. Side-by-side with West Berkshire Council, the Trust aims to create a place where wildlife can thrive and which people can enjoy too.

15
❧ DAUBENTON'S BAT ❧

If you catch a glimpse of a fast, agile bat swooping down over a pond in the moonlight, there is a good chance it's a Daubenton's bat – also known as the 'water bat' since they rely heavily on water and aquatic insects for food.

Daubenton's bats have unusually large, furry feet which they use to grab mosquitos and moths from the water's surface. In summer, they may roost in tree hollows or attics, but in the cold winter months they retreat to underground caves or tunnels to hibernate.

During the 20th century, the number of bats found in Britain decreased at an alarming rate, with some species declining by over 50%. Daubenton's and other bat species have been recorded on many of BBOWT's wooded and waterside nature reserves. These wildlife havens are managed to provide good foraging grounds for bats, and local volunteers have helped to convert old structures, like pillboxes and tunnels, into cool and sheltered hibernation sites.

16

‿ DOWNY EMERALD ‿

Downy emerald dragonflies occur mostly in the south-east of England, but are not common, and continuing losses of acidic woodland pools leave them vulnerable. In our three counties, suitable habitat is only found in the south and east of Berkshire.

A part-shaded woodland or heathland pond in May and June can be a chaotic scene, with four-spotted chasers 'living fast', but you may be lucky enough to see a darker, more methodical dragonfly patrolling a beat low to the water – this is the dazzling downy emerald with its metallic green eyes and thorax, and dark, bronzy abdomen. The patrolling males have a pinched waist and hold their abdomen with a slight arch.

At Decoy Heath, an old silted pond was recently re-excavated by volunteers and already downy emeralds have begun to reappear. At Wildmoor Heath meanwhile, a new woodland pond is planned principally for downy emerald conservation.

17

❧ DUKE OF BURGUNDY ❧

This small, orange and brown-chequered butterfly is an elusive creature, often only glimpsed as it darts around the leaves of sunlight-dappled primroses on our Dancersend Nature Reserve. Nationally, this butterfly has suffered serious declines over the past 50 years as its favourite habitats – chalk grassland and clearings in ancient woodlands – have been lost.

At Dancersend work to help the Duke of Burgundy was started by the great naturalist and pioneer conservationist, Miriam Rothschild whose family once owned the estate. This has been faithfully continued; areas of chalk grassland and scrub are being kept open and a small population of this rare butterfly is clinging on.

Thanks to the work of dedicated volunteers, we have managed to gain an understanding of the needs of this species which has helped to inform careful scrub management and grazing around the reserve. By working alongside neighbouring landowners, it is hoped that this noble butterfly will be able to expand into the surrounding countryside, too.

18

~ EXTINGUISHER MOSS ~

Being no more than two centimetres tall, the extinguisher moss is often overlooked. But if you take a closer look, you'll see that it is indeed very pretty and you might spot what gives it its name – tiny hooded caps that look like candle-snuffers covering the fruiting capsules which protrude from the main tuft of leaves on upright red stalks.

An uncommon moss of limestone areas in Oxfordshire and Buckinghamshire, it prefers to grow on thin soil found on dry stone walls and in limestone quarries. But these habitats are under threat; quarries are often overgrown by scrub and other, taller plants, while dry stone walls fall into disrepair because they are no longer seen as necessary for agriculture.

Luckily, the extinguisher moss is safe at two BBOWT reserves: Hitchcopse Pit, where hundreds, clinging to the shallow soil on the cliff edge, benefit from BBOWT's traditional management techniques to keep the cliff walls scrub free; and Hook Norton Cutting, where it grows with other rare mosses on the embankments of this old railway cutting.

19

❧ GREAT BURNET ❧

Our area is a national stronghold for floodplain meadows; it is synonymous with fields filled with wildflowers, the hum of insects in summer and the haunting cry of the curlew. These special grasslands have thrived, often for centuries, thanks to the way they are traditionally managed which results in a flower-rich hay crop.

For conservationists, the presence of great burnet indicates that a rare group of wild flowers and grasses may be flourishing on these meadows. This member of the rose family, with its deep crimson flowers, can survive several decades thanks to its extensive root system. But changes in agriculture, and increased drainage over the past 70 years, have seen most of our floodplain meadows disappear.

Only 1,600 hectares now remain – an area only a third of the size of Oxford – making it an international priority for protection. But BBOWT is safeguarding this habitat at reserves such as Oxey Mead, Iffley Meadows, Chimney Meadows and the Upper Ray Meadows.

20

∽ GREAT CRESTED NEWT ∽

In times past, the great crested newt, also known as the 'warty newt', would have lived in natural wetland habitats across northern Europe. Over time, human activity, including the drainage of the land for agriculture, closely followed by the loss of man-made ponds through development, has resulted in the disappearance of many wetlands. These changes in our landscape have taken their toll on great crested newts to the extent that they now receive the highest level of legal protection.

We are fortunate in Britain to have one of the strongest populations of great crested newts in Europe. They are particularly fond of lowland farmland and old quarries, and so are found throughout our three counties. Kintbury Newt Ponds is one of this dragon-like newt's favourite spots and was saved from development in the late 1990s. BBOWT continues to work closely with planners to raise awareness of protected species and help ensure important habitats are safeguarded.

❧ GREAT GREEN BUSH-CRICKET ❧

Great and green is certainly an appropriate name for this impressive insect; one of Britain's largest. Adults reach over five centimetres in length and are a bright green colour all over except for a brown stripe along the back. The males produce a loud, electronic-sounding song by rubbing special parts of their forewings together. You might think that such a large, noisy insect would be easy to spot, but it's expertly camouflaged and it's very hard to pinpoint the origin of the male's song.

The great green bush-cricket lives on grassland dotted with patches of scrub. It prefers light, dry soils into which the females can lay their eggs in summer using their long, down-curved ovipositors. Great green bush-crickets can be found at our Dry Sandford Pit and Warren Bank nature reserves where such mosaics of grass and scrub are maintained. Surprisingly, these bush-crickets are omnivorous, eating other insects as well as vegetation. They are also capable of giving humans a painful nip!

22
❧ GREEN TIGER BEETLE ❧

When someone says the words 'voracious predator', a shiny green beetle may not be the first animal that comes to mind. But if you take a closer look at this spectacular insect, you'll see a ferocious pair of jaws, giving a clue to its carnivorous appetite. The distinctive iridescent green body with yellow-cream spots sits on top of a set of six long legs, which give the beetle an impressive turn of speed – it is one of Britain's fastest insect runners. This mini-tiger uses its speed to hunt other invertebrates, such as spiders and ants.

The sun-loving green tiger beetle can be found on sunny, dry soils such as those of heathland. At Wildmoor Heath and Decoy Heath, it enjoys the open aspect maintained by preventing scrub encroachment which would shade out the heath. The larvae of the beetle make burrows in the sandy soil, waiting at the entrance ready to ambush any prey that passes close by.

23

❧ GREEN-WINGED ORCHID ❧

Fields coloured with the purple of green-winged orchids were once a common sight across much of Britain. With flowers that are typically purple (although sometimes pale pink), and the pair of green-veined 'wing' sepals that it is named for; this orchid's decline reflects the wider loss of wildflower meadows from our countryside.

The loss of this pretty flower is almost entirely due to changes in farming practices over the last 50 years. This orchid favours damp, unimproved grassland – a habitat which has become increasingly rare as meadows have been drained, ploughed and treated with fertilisers, making conditions unsuitable for many species that once thrived.

But there is still hope. Careful management and restoration of remaining areas of unimproved grassland provides strongholds where meadow flowers such as this can flourish. Between late April and mid-June, those visiting reserves such as Pilch Field, Chimney Meadows and Bernwood Meadows, can continue to admire its purple blooms.

24
∽ HAZEL DORMOUSE ∽

With its golden fur, thick fluffy tail, long whiskers and large black eyes, the hazel dormouse must be one of our most endearing mammals. Renowned for its sleeping abilities, it is nocturnal and hibernates through the winter.

Once widespread, dormice are now sadly extinct from around half of their former haunts. Local populations are mainly confined to woodlands in the Chilterns where our reserves are being carefully managed with dormice in mind, and nest boxes provide safe refuges.

The dormice living at Little Linford Wood have a particularly special story to tell; they've been on quite a journey… In 1998, they were unwittingly living in the path of the Channel Tunnel Rail Link in Kent. Needing to be re-homed, they were captured and released into the safe haven of Little Linford Wood as part of a national reintroduction programme. The dormice clearly approved of their new home and are today continuing to thrive and spread into neighbouring areas.

25
❧ HERB-PARIS ❧

With its whorl of four egg-shaped leaves, herb-Paris is known as the 'herb of equality' as all its parts are considered equal and harmonious. This symmetry appealed to medieval herbalists who used the plant in a complex ritual to help young girls conjure up images of their future husbands.

Herb-Paris is a perennial herb of moist, calcareous, ancient woodland and its understated flowers may be found in the spring amongst spectacular carpets of bluebells, violets and primroses. It flowers and fruits most freely when an area in the woodland is opened up after coppicing, but also persists in deep shade. It is used by conservationists as an indicator of ancient woodland and can be found alongside dog's mercury and moschatel, which are also reliable pointers to the ancient history of woodlands. Herb-Paris can be found at Bowdown Woods, Warburg, Foxholes, Sydlings Copse and Little Linford Wood nature reserves, to name just a few.

26

⊰ KINGFISHER ⊱

The kingfisher's striking mix of iridescent turquoise and metallic copper is instantly recognisable as an iconic symbol of British rivers. But being the size of a sparrow makes this riverside favourite harder to spot than you would expect; usually their distinctive shrill call is heard before they are seen flying low over the water.

Kingfishers breed near lowland watercourses which have suitable banks for burrowing nests and shallow edges for feeding. Moor Copse and College Lake provide ideal habitats for these brilliantly coloured birds. But there's something a little different at Haymill Valley… Two giant metal kingfisher sculptures mirror the wildlife on site as part of a local art project.

It was once thought that owning the feathers of a kingfisher was a good luck charm. But the luck of the kingfisher is diminishing as their numbers decline due to the pollution of rivers and streams. BBOWT is working with many partners to provide the best riverside habitat for kingfishers and other, water-loving creatures.

27
~ LAPWING ~

This handsome bird is easily recognisable in flight by the broad, bluntly rounded shape of its wings and its distinctive flapping. Males perform impressive twisting dives in tumbling courtship flights, accompanied by their evocative 'pee-wit' calls. From a distance, the lapwing's plumage may appear to simply be a striking combination of black and white, but if you get a closer look, the black wings have an iridescent green and purple sheen. Added to these attractive colours, the birds have an extravagant crest on the back of their heads.

Once very common, the lapwing has suffered a serious decline in numbers over recent years as a result of changes in land use and farming practices. These ground-nesting birds need low-disturbance areas for breeding, such as the islands specially created in the marsh at College Lake. Large winter flocks of lapwing can also be seen at Chimney Meadows, where the wet meadows provide abundant feeding grounds.

28

❧ MARSH HELLEBORINE ❧

The marsh helleborine is a stunning orchid of wetland areas. It has a rather loose flower spike, with up to 20 large white and pink flowers, seen in July and August. One of the real spectacles of the year at Dry Sandford Pit is the display of marsh helleborines in flower. In most other areas of the country, this orchid is declining, especially in southern England where the draining of wetlands has had a major impact. But at Dry Sandford Pit this trend has been bucked and hundreds of flowers make up the breathtaking display.

The open nature of Dry Sandford Pit (a mix of grassland and fenland) and the limey springwater are the most likely reasons for the impressive display, as the marsh helleborine likes to be out in the sunlight but rooted in damp ground. There has been a big increase in numbers over the past few years as more areas of the reserve have been opened up through scrub removal.

29
✎ MILITARY ORCHID ✎

So named because the flowers resemble a tiny soldier complete with legs, arms, a buttoned jacket and even a helmet, the military orchid was a common sight on the chalk of southern England up to the mid-19th century. But it began to disappear, becoming extinct in county after county, until in the early part of the 20th century it had all but gone from the south.

In May of 1947, the eminent naturalist J.E. Lousley stopped in the Chilterns for a picnic and stumbled across the orchid just coming into flower. Due to the threat of orchid collectors, however, he never made its location public.

It wasn't until the 1960s that the colony was found once again at Homefield Wood. The discovery was communicated by a now famous telegram that simply read: "The soldiers are safe in their home field." Thanks to the watchful eyes of volunteers, these orchids have risen from just six plants in 1977 to over 200 today. As they flourish, we are now able to encourage visitors to view these remarkable flowers.

30
∾ MONKEY ORCHID ∾

If you happen to be walking across the sunny, chalk grassland slopes of Hartslock in May, be sure to cast your eyes down from the beautiful views of the River Thames. For there, spreading out before you, is a carpet of flowering monkey orchids. As its name suggests, this monkey-like, rare flower with its 'tail' and long 'limbs' is sure to bring a smile to your face. But it is a shocking fact that it is found in merely a handful of locations in Britain.

During the 1800s, populations suffered drastically due to collectors and the ploughing and planting of suitable habitat; the monkey orchid was believed to be extinct. Miraculously rediscovered in Kent in the 1950s, there are now only three current populations including Hartslock. With invaluable input from passionate volunteers, BBOWT manages this incredible legacy. The good news is that numbers are increasing – from eight plants in 1977 to well over 450 today.

31
❧ NIGHTJAR ❧

It is a sound that you never forget; listening to the distinctive churring of a male nightjar on a balmy summer evening is just captivating. Getting to see one, though, can be another matter. Superbly camouflaged by their grey-brown mottled plumage, nightjars nest on the ground amongst heather and scrub. On its Berkshire reserves, BBOWT has been working hard to increase the amount of nightjar habitat by clearing 'fingers' into the scrub and trees. This creates open areas and encourages nightjars to breed.

Nesting on the ground means that nightjars are sensitive to disturbance. The parents can be scared off their nests by walkers, and particularly by their dogs, leaving the eggs vulnerable to predators such as crows. A reduction in suitable breeding habitat and feeding areas contributed to their massive decline in the 1980s. More recent increases are attributed to large-scale felling of plantations, but are being offset by decreased breeding success as a result of disturbance.

32
ꝏ OTTER ꝏ

A distant splash, a shape slipping through the water…If you're lucky you may have caught a glimpse of one of the UK's most charismatic mammals – the otter. Reaching an impressive length of up to 1.5 metres, their streamlined bodies and water-resistant fur coat, make them perfectly adapted for a life of fishing in our rivers.

Sadly, due to water pollution, habitat loss and poisoning by pesticides, the numbers of otters in the UK declined dramatically during the second half of the 20th century. By the 1970s, the otter had become extinct from our three counties and much of England.

The offending chemicals were banned and a major programme to improve the state of our rivers, overseen by the Environment Agency, had a dramatic effect. By the 1990s, otters had begun to spread from the few areas where they had managed to cling on. BBOWT worked with the agency, landowners, angling clubs and volunteers to restore suitable habitat to help otters spread. Today, we are lucky to have these delightful animals back in our region.

33

✌ PALE DOG-VIOLET ∿

The narrow leaves of this diminutive flower could be easily overlooked or mistaken for one of its more common relatives. When its milky-violet flowers emerge in May, however, it reveals itself to be a beautiful heathland gem.

Sadly, this pretty flower is becoming increasingly rare. Populations have been hit by the destruction and fragmentation of their precious heathland habitat. In fact, over 80% of lowland heathland has been lost in the UK in just 200 years. Despite this loss, BBOWT has protected and increased the only known population in the three counties at its stunning Inkpen Common Nature Reserve in Berkshire.

This delicate flower struggles to grow under the shade of trees and amongst thorny scrub. This means that it enjoys the clearings created by our local volunteer team and flourishes when these are grazed by New Forest ponies. This has helped to increase the population from the low hundreds in the 1990s to over 2,000 in 2005.

34
❧ PORCELAIN FUNGUS ❧

Beechwoods in autumn are magical places – the beech leaves turning from green to golden yellow, the crunch of fallen leaves underfoot, the earthy autumn smell, and above all, mysterious fungi emerging from beneath the fallen leaves, or growing in delicate tufts on fallen wood and on the trees themselves.

One such fungus, sometimes appearing high up on the beech trunks, is the delicately translucent porcelain fungus. Although not rare, the slimy white caps grow in small tufts only on beech trees and can be seen on many of BBOWTs Chiltern nature reserves, such as Warburg. Away from the Chilterns, Foxholes in the far west of Oxfordshire is particularly rich in beechwood fungi, where the porcelain fungus looks down from on high at bright red beechwood sickeners and purple amethyst deceivers, dotted, jewel-like amongst the leaf litter. In many of these woodlands BBOWT leaves standing and fallen dead wood which not only supports the fungi growing on them, but is also home to a multitude of minibeasts.

35

ى PURPLE EMPEROR ى

One of the summer treats at Finemere Wood is the sight of a purple emperor. You might catch a glimpse of a large powerful outline coasting over the tops of the oak trees along the rides, or get a rare close-up of one basking on the bare patches on the ground. You may even be lucky enough to spot one alight on a goat willow, curve its abdomen underneath the leaf that it stands on and lay a tiny white egg.

Once part of the Royal Forest of Bernwood, Finemere Wood is true emperor habitat. For centuries the woodland was managed for coppice, providing wood for tools, fires and furniture. The presence of the purple emperor today (a species which declined in the 20th century) is a reminder of why we still manage our woodland willows carefully; rotational coppicing ensures that there is always a good supply of young willows growing on the sunny ride edges.

36
✍ QUAKING GRASS ✍

Gently shivering in the breeze, the loose heads of quaking grass are a distinctive feature of our meadows and grasslands. Heart-shaped flowers dance on delicate stems, giving the plant its many names from totter grass to shakky-tremmels, dithery dock to dothery dick!

The habitats that this pretty grass favours are gradually disappearing as our traditional hay meadows make way for agricultural intensification and our chalk grasslands disappear under scrub. BBOWT is working hard to protect these places, however. At Chimney Meadows the generosity of members and public alike helped us to buy an extension where work to convert the arable fields into flower-rich meadows has been underway. These meadows are now resplendent in summer, showcasing a whole host of plants including quaking grass.

The restoration of Chimney Meadows has not only helped our fading wild flowers, but insects now buzz in the fields, yellowhammers visit the seeds, hares bound in the fields and voles nibble at the grasses, hiding from kestrels hovering overhead.

37
⤷ RAGGED-ROBIN ⤶

The pink, frayed flowers of ragged-robin are a familiar image of wildflower meadows, but this delicate plant is declining. As farming becomes more intensive and our wetlands are drained to make way for development, the places where this well-known flower can survive are fast disappearing.

But the story of ragged-robin doesn't end there – work to restore our meadows is providing hope that they can not only continue to exist, but be havens for wildlife. At BBOWT nature reserves such as Asham Meads, Pilch Field and Woodsides Meadow, wetland features are being restored and wild flowers are being encouraged by hay-cutting, grazing and spreading local seed. And the result? Meadows ablaze with colour in summer, from the pink of ragged-robin to the deep red of great burnet and sunshine gold of yellow rattle. A trip to see these ancient meadows, where traditional ploughs have left old ridge and furrow marks, is a trip back in time.

38
∽ REED BUNTING ∽

Emblematic of wetlands and, more recently, farmland, reed buntings favour areas with dense vegetation. The handsome male has a distinctive black head, white collar and drooping white moustache. Characteristically, he perches high on reeds, rushes or scrub to voice his simple three-note territorial call. But since the 1970s, the UK's breeding population of reed buntings has declined dramatically by 67% to only 200,000 pairs. Detrimental changes have occurred to our wetland habitats; many have been extensively drained for agriculture and urban development.

Chimney Meadows lies in one of the best wetland areas in England. The wet habitats along the River Thames boast up to 70 pairs of reed bunting through the breeding season. Other key reserves for reed buntings include Lashford Lane Fen, Western Turville and the Loddon. By maintaining reedbeds, creating new wetlands and encouraging initiatives promoting spring-sown cereals in farmland, BBOWT hopes to aid a recovery of reed buntings.

39

✑ ROUND-LEAVED SUNDEW ✑

Amongst the soggy sphagnum mosses of the valley bogs at Wildmoor Heath there lives a strange and beautiful plant. Its flowers are white, delicate and pretty enough… But it's really its leaves that give the sundew its beauty, and its diet that makes it stand out from the crowd.

The round-leaved sundew has a rosette of green leaves on long, red stalks. On each leaf there are lots of hair-like tendrils, tipped with droplets that glisten in the sun. Insects are attracted to this 'dew' but it is very sticky. When the sundew's 'hairs' sense the presence of prey, they curl inwards holding the insect tight. Eventually the whole leaf curls over and the enclosed insect is digested, its nutrients absorbed by the plant.

By protecting our rare wet heathland and bog habitats, BBOWT is helping to ensure the survival of this fascinating plant – a careful regime of grazing and scrub-cutting prevents the heathland from being smothered by more vigorous plants.

40
⌇ RUBY-TAILED WASP ⌇

The beautifully metallic ruby-tailed wasp is an example of the many species of solitary bee and wasp which have been recorded at Dry Sandford Pit. These insects do not live in colonies like honey bees and bumblebees, but instead the female builds a nest by herself, stocks it with pollen and lays an egg within each cell.

At Dry Sandford Pit the low cliff faces of soft Jurassic rock are ideal for the females to dig their nests in and, if kept exposed and clear of encroaching vegetation, the cliff wall provides warmth for larvae to develop successfully. Other species also use their environment ingeniously to provide shelter – the tawny mining bee digs its nest in lawns and leaf-cutter bees cut neat circles from leaves and petals to build their nests. Solitary bees and wasps are excellent pollinators and since they often only use one flower species for nectar, maintaining floral diversity is critical to their survival.

41
❧ SCARLET TIGER MOTH ❧

Hear the word 'moth' and you are more likely to think in dull, muted browns than in bright, primary hues, but these fascinating creatures come in all shades and sizes. You don't need to wait until nightfall to see the more striking species, either. The scarlet tiger moth is the perfect example of a day-flying variety, as stunning as the very best dressed butterflies. With its punchy black, white and yellow markings underlain with a brazenly bright blaze of red, this distinctive insect typically appears in midsummer, fluttering around riverbanks, marshes and fens.

At Moor Copse in Berkshire, BBOWT has been managing the riverbanks to ensure that comfrey can flourish – one of the main food plants for the larvae of this moth. Meanwhile, Parsonage Moor in Oxfordshire has been the location of a study into the genetics of the scarlet tiger moth which has generated over 50 years' worth of data!

42
❧ SILVER-STUDDED BLUE ❧

Neglected, scrubbed over, fragmented, and built on; this has been the fate of many of southern England's once extensive heathland habitats.

This decline has occurred as the heaths have ceased to provide economic benefits to local people. Products such as timber for fuel or building, animal fodder and bedding, food and medicines were all taken from heathland. These uses resulted in large tracts of heath being kept open and not 'improved' with the use of fertilisers, resulting in low, young heather growth and plenty of hot, bare ground – ideal conditions for the silver-studded blue butterfly.

The silver-studded blue gets its name from dots of light blue reflective scales found on the underside of the wings of the adults. Sadly, during the last 10 years, it has declined rapidly and has even disappeared from two BBOWT nature reserves. It now only remains at Broadmoor Bottom (part of Wildmoor Heath), where targeted scrub-cutting and grazing have provided the right conditions to help it to survive.

43
ᴥ SKYLARK ᴥ

The skylark has featured in many works of literature and music due to its unrivalled song-flight. The male rises almost vertically with rapid wing-beats, effortlessly hovers and sings from a great height, and then parachutes back down to earth. Song-flights can last for up to one hour, and the birds can reach 300 metres before descending.

Unfortunately, one of the most evocative sounds of a British summer's day is now far less common. Over the last 30 years, skylark numbers have declined by a massive 90%, mostly due to changes in farming practices.

Despite this national decline, BBOWT has been able to increase breeding numbers on several of its reserves through sympathetic habitat management. At Wells Farm, the growing of spring-sown crops, the leaving of winter stubble and the provision of field margins and beetle banks, has allowed visitors to continue to marvel at the sound of an 'exaltation of skylarks'.

44

❧ SMALL RED DAMSELFLY ❧

The dainty but graceful small red damselfly is one of our smallest damselflies. Despite its blood-red coloration, it is surprisingly camouflaged as it flits and settles amongst the grasses and rushes fringing its favoured pools and bogs.

The small red is a scarce species in the UK, with a restricted distribution. It is normally found on lowland heathland and will only fly on the sunniest, warmest and calmest days. But when the adults are on the wing, between June and August, keep an eye out for their unusual hunting technique; they fly and bump into plants in an effort to flush prey out for their next meal.

BBOWT is helping to maintain the populations of small red damselflies on its Berkshire heathland reserves, such as Decoy Heath and Wildmoor Heath, by keeping encroaching shading trees in check and maintaining their favoured shallow acidic pools and flashes, allowing this unassuming but charismatic little gem to thrive.

45

∽ SNAKE'S-HEAD FRITILLARY ∾

It was not so long ago that Covent Garden's flower markets were overflowing with the delicate, nodding pink and white blooms of the snake's-head fritillary. Handfuls picked from the meadows beside the River Thames, were taken by local children down to London to fetch a pretty penny or two.

Eventually, the once-common sight of carpets of pink stretching out along the river became rarer; our wildflower meadows began to disappear at an alarming rate. But one place has managed to buck the trend. With careful love and attention, the snake's-head fritillaries at Iffley Meadows have grown in number from only 500 plants when the reserve was taken over in 1983 to an astounding 42,000 plants today – a fact we know as every year, volunteers and staff carefully count them. A combination of the right grazing and management has helped Iffley Meadows thrive. And every April, these delightful flowers push their way through the soil to herald spring and take the breath away of any passer-by.

46

❧ SOUTHERN DAMSELFLY ❧

Southern damselflies are extremely rare and legally protected in Britain, with strongholds in the New Forest and Pembrokeshire, many miles from our region. By rights, as extremely weak fliers, these delicate damselflies shouldn't be in our three counties at all, but here they are! Although the origins of this species in Oxfordshire remain shrouded in mystery, their current status is clear, with populations at Dry Sandford Pit and Parsonage Moor going from strength to strength.

At first glance, these blue damselflies can look much like the many other small blue damselflies, but closer investigation will reveal their unique tiny black 'viking helmet' mark.

Southern damselflies are particularly fussy about where they live, preferring to set up home in shallow, gently flowing, chalky streams. Careful management using ponies to graze vegetation and opening up water-filled channels has provided the perfect real estate for this species; so much so, that a glimpse of this rare damselfly is almost guaranteed.

47

❧ STRIPED LYCHNIS MOTH ❧

Warburg Nature Reserve provides a home to a treasure trove of insects, including the striped lychnis moth. Following widespread decline throughout much of the countryside, appropriate management of chalk grassland sites, like Warburg, are crucial to secure the long-term survival of this species.

While the adult moth is rarely encountered, the brightly coloured caterpillars can be found much more easily. They feed on the developing flowers and seeds of dark mullein; by patiently searching these plants in August and September it is possible to see them. But spotters beware! The caterpillars of the mullein moth are very similar. Striped lychnis caterpillars generally have a clear band of pale green between segments with no black spots – these only appear on the caterpillars of the mullein moth. Quite incredibly, striped lychnis caterpillars pupate in a cocoon on or just below the soil surface, and can remain in this state for three or four winters, before emerging as adult moths.

48
⚬ WATER VOLE ⚬

Immortalised as Ratty in the children's classic, *The Wind in the Willows*, the water vole is the largest and most famous of our vole species. "As he looked it winked at him… a brown little face, with whiskers. A grave round face… small neat ears and thick silky hair," wrote Kenneth Grahame in 1908, reportedly inspired by watching water voles on the River Pang in Berkshire.

But since this time, water voles have declined dramatically, disappearing from an estimated 95% of sites. This decline has mainly been the result of habitat damage or loss, coupled with the spread of an introduced predator, the American mink. To help protect this charismatic species, the Water Vole Recovery Project was established by BBOWT and the Environment Agency. Over the last decade, the project has been working hard to conserve our local water voles so that future generations may continue to enjoy seeing Ratty doing what he loves most: "messing about on the river".

49
~ WIGEON ~

The colourful chestnut, pink and grey wigeon is a sociable duck, and one of many waterbirds that have benefited from wetlands carefully managed by BBOWT. These pretty birds can be spotted in their hundreds, dabbling in close groups or flying in tight-knit formations over the waters of College Lake, with a glorious backdrop of the Chiltern Hills.

College Lake, once a noisy chalk quarry, is now a tranquil haven for wildlife thanks to the dedication of a band of volunteers. Accessible to all, relaxed trails and numerous bird hides provide stunning views down on to the waters of the lake and marsh.

BBOWT carries out a whole host of work on its wetland sites – from creating new ponds and scrapes for wildfowl and wading birds, to re-profiling rivers and streams to encourage water voles. Work is carefully planned to provide ideal feeding or nesting opportunities, and often benefits a whole host of animals, plants and insects.

50
❧ WILD SERVICE-TREE ❧

The wild service-tree, inconspicuous for much of the year, has a regal history. Once widespread, if seldom abundant, it grew in the forests which covered England and Wales. But as the woodlands were cleared, it disappeared from our countryside. It is now found in ancient woodlands and hedges, such as those of former royal hunting forests, where wild boar may well have helped disperse its seed.

Locally, wild service-trees are found in the ancient Forest of Bernwood. Amongst the planted conifers, the splashes of scarlet among the dark evergreens are dramatic. At Finemere Wood there are only a few wild service-trees to be found but they can be easily spotted by their beautiful white blossom in May or the magnificent crimson leaves in autumn. BBOWT works to ensure that ancient woodlands are protected and positively managed so that species like the wild service-tree can continue to survive.

_1_ ADDER
PICTURE: John Cancalosi/naturepl.com
WORDS: Giles Alder

_2_ BADGER
PICTURE: Andrew Parkinson/naturepl.com
WORDS: Rachel Martin

_3_ BARN OWL
PICTURE: Danny Green/rspb-images
WORDS: Colin Williams

_4_ BLACK HAIRSTREAK
PICTURE: Jim Asher
WORDS: Debbie Lewis

_5_ BLACKENING WAXCAP
PICTURE: Lasse Christensen/flickr
WORDS: Peter Creed

_11_ CORN BUNTING
PICTURE: R. Usher/4nature
WORDS: Martyn Lane

_12_ CORNCOCKLE
PICTURE: Helen Walsh
WORDS: Nancy Reed

_13_ CURLEW
PICTURE: David Morris
WORDS: Mick A'Court

_14_ DARTFORD WARBLER
PICTURE: davidkjaer.com
WORDS: Jacky Akam

_15_ DAUBENTON'S BAT
PICTURE: Dietmar Nill/naturepl.com
WORDS: Julia Armstrong

_21_ GREAT GREEN BUSH-CRICKET
PICTURE: Thijs van Balen Jr.
WORDS: Andy Fairbairn

_22_ GREEN TIGER BEETLE
PICTURE: J. Héras/4nature
WORDS: Andy Fairbairn

_23_ GREEN-WINGED ORCHID
PICTURE: Colin Varndell
WORDS: Stacey Hewitt

_24_ HAZEL DORMOUSE
PICTURE: davidkjaer.com
WORDS: Julia Armstrong

_25_ HERB-PARIS
PICTURE: Peter Creed
WORDS: Maggie Piggott

_31_ NIGHTJAR
PICTURE: David Tipling/rspb-images
WORDS: Jenni Hignett

_32_ OTTER
PICTURE: Helen Walsh
WORDS: Erin Murton

_33_ PALE DOG-VIOLET
PICTURE: Peter Creed
WORDS: Ian Stevenson

_34_ PORCELAIN FUNGUS
PICTURE: Peter Creed
WORDS: Peter Creed

_35_ PURPLE EMPEROR
PICTURE: Peter Eeles
WORDS: Giles Strother

_41_ SCARLET TIGER MOTH
PICTURE: Peter Creed
WORDS: Claire Baylis

_42_ SILVER-STUDDED BLUE
PICTURE: Jim Asher
WORDS: Andy Coulson-Phillips

_43_ SKYLARK
PICTURE: Markus Varesvuo/birdphoto.fi
WORDS: Colin Williams

_44_ SMALL RED DAMSELFLY
PICTURE: Kate Dent
WORDS: Colin Williams

_45_ SNAKE'S-HEAD FRITILLARY
PICTURE: Helen Walsh
WORDS: Helen Walsh

6 BLUEBELL
PICTURE: Colin Varndell
WORDS: Brian Miller

7 BULLFINCH
PICTURE: Steve Knell/rspb-images
WORDS: Helen d'Ayala

8 CHALKHILL BLUE
PICTURE: davidkjaer.com
WORDS: Debbie Lewis

9 CHILTERN GENTIAN
PICTURE: Peter Creed
WORDS: Giles Strother

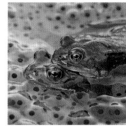

10 COMMON FROG
PICTURE: Joe Blossom/nhpa
WORDS: Claire Baylis

16 DOWNY EMERALD
PICTURE: Ville Airo/flickr
WORDS: Andy Coulson-Phillips

17 DUKE OF BURGUNDY
PICTURE: Andy Sands/naturepl.com
WORDS: Mark Vallance

18 EXTINGUISHER MOSS
PICTURE: Peter Creed
WORDS: Wolfgang Ritter

19 GREAT BURNET
PICTURE: Lisa J. R. Williams
WORDS: Matthew Chambers

20 GREAT CRESTED NEWT
PICTURE: davidkjaer.com
WORDS: Rebecca Micklem

26 KINGFISHER
PICTURE: davidkjaer.com
WORDS: Louise Print-Lyons

27 LAPWING
PICTURE: Markus Varesvuo/birdphoto.fi
WORDS: Andy Fairbairn

28 MARSH HELLEBORINE
PICTURE: Peter Creed
WORDS: Martyn Lane

29 MILITARY ORCHID
PICTURE: Helen Walsh
WORDS: Mark Vallance

30 MONKEY ORCHID
PICTURE: Gavin Hageman
WORDS: Nicole Clough

36 QUAKING GRASS
PICTURE: John Martin/fotoflora.com
WORDS: Helen Walsh

37 RAGGED-ROBIN
PICTURE: Peter Creed
WORDS: Helen Walsh

38 REED BUNTING
PICTURE: Alan Williams/nhpa
WORDS: Kerry Lock

39 ROUND-LEAVED SUNDEW
PICTURE: Kate Dent
WORDS: Abby Stephens

40 RUBY-TAILED WASP
PICTURE: Goldenorfe/flickr
WORDS: Pim Young

46 SOUTHERN DAMSELFLY
PICTURE: Peter Creed
WORDS: Debbie Lewis

47 STRIPED LYCHNIS MOTH
PICTURE: David G. Green
WORDS: Kelly Thomas

48 WATER VOLE
PICTURE: Terry Longley/seeing.org.uk
WORDS: Julia Armstrong

49 WIGEON
PICTURE: davidkjaer.com
WORDS: Roger Stace

50 WILD SERVICE-TREE
PICTURE: Peter Creed
WORDS: Lisa Lane

A gift in your Will – protect wildlife for the future

To find out more visit **www.bbowt.org.uk** or call **01865 775476**

"My wife and I recently updated
our Wills to include leaving a
legacy to BBOWT. It seemed an
ideal way of giving something
back, while helping to maintain
these wonderful landscapes."
Steve Woolliams, 51, Oxford